by Maryann Dobeck   illustrated by Lindy Burnett

Orlando   Boston   Dallas   Chicago   San Diego

Visit *The Learning Site!*

www.harcourtschool.com

ISBN 0-15-325407-6

7 8 9 10 121 10 09 08 07 06 05 04

Ordering Options
ISBN 0-15-323766-X (Collection)
ISBN 0-15-329523-6 (package of 5)

the popcorn

2

the balloons

the pie

4

the milk

the hats

the juice

the party!